68 YEARS BEHIND THE PLOW
My Journey from the Farm to the Pulpit

by
Forrest Tyndall Chapman

Copyright © 2018 by Forrest T. Chapman

All rights reserved.
First Printing, 2018

ISBN 13: 978-1-98361-080-6
ISBN 10: 1-98361-080-1

Contact:
Chappie1929@gmail.com

ALL PHOTOS ARE FROM THE PERSONAL COLLECTION OF FORREST CHAPMAN
WITH THE EXCEPTION OF THOSE LISTED BELOW

ATTRIBUTION FOR THE FOLLOWING IMAGES:

Plow photo - Cover: canacopegdl.com
Adair P. Chapman obituary – Dedication: DallasMorningNews.com and legacy.com
Farm graphic – Table of Contents: canstockphoto.com
Preacher/Pulpit graphic – Table of Contents: weclipart.com
Farmer and Mule Plowing graphic – Table of Contents: mozira.com
Old wood stove photo – p8: i.pinimg.com
Harding College Sign photo – p13: alumnius.net/univerphotos/
Dr. George S. Benson photo – p13: encyclopediaofarkansas.net
West End Church of Christ photo – p17: the westender.com
Dawson Road Church of Christ photo – p17: dawsonroad.org
GACS Groundbreaking photo – p42: myschoolcdn.com/bbklzel-cdn
Ferry photo – p44: i.pinimg.com
Moonshine/still photo – 45: i.pinimg.com
Baptism in the River – p46: i.pinimg.com
JJ & Isabelle Turner photo – p53: mcdonoughcofc.org
World Bible Institute graphic – p53: worldbibleinstitute.com
PFC Lamar Calvin Howell photo – p61: vvmf.org
Ranew Gravesite photo – p63: findagrave.com
Charles O'Neal photo – p64: valdostadailytimes.com
Masada photo – p66: pixabay.com
Romania photo – p67: pixabay.com
Harvey Starling photo – p68: theLordsway.com/cedargrovecofc/
Trinidad food photo – p68: i.pinimg.com

*"I've learned that people will forget what you said,
people will forget what you did,
but people will never forget how you made them feel."*

Maya Angelou

Dedication

I wish to dedicate this book in memory of my brother, Adair P. Chapman, Jr. Without his encouragement and constant counsel, I never would have begun or survived as a minister. Adair lived most of his life in Dallas, TX with his beloved wife, Nancy, and preached for some of the largest congregations in our brotherhood. He began an effective Way of the Cross mission ministry in the Midwest. We worked together in Kansas, Indiana and Missouri a few times. He passed to his reward on July 12, 2013.

Adair Pinckney Chapman, Jr. passed into glory on July 12, 2013, in Dallas, at age 92. He is survived by Nancy, beloved wife of 72 years, two children, two grandchildren and one great-

grandchild. Born in Berlin, Ga., and a graduate of Harding College, he became superintendent of schools in Knobel, Ark., at age 21. Adair entered ministry in the mission fields of Georgia and Kentucky and later became minister at established congregations in Kansas City, KN, Port Arthur, TX and Dallas, TX. In 1980, he created a charitable organization, First Century Way of the Cross Ministry, and began one of the first prison ministries in our nation including the largest tape ministry at that time. Adair's heart burned with an urgent call to lost and forgotten souls. He was instrumental in planting and strengthening many rural churches across the South and Midwest that continue the Lord's work today.

Introduction

In reflecting over 68 years of preaching there have been countless friends who have given me encouragement in local and, especially, mission work. Without them and the congregations, I would have never accomplished much as a preacher. Within these pages you will find the names of some whom I place in the "Hall of Fame." The pages in this book are my memories and reflections of almost seven decades of ministry. It is my desire that you will benefit from reading it as much as I have from writing it.

"However, I consider my life worth nothing to me; my only aim is to finish the race and complete the task the Lord Jesus has given me— the task of testifying to the good news of God's grace."
Acts 20:24

68 YEARS BEHIND THE PLOW
My Journey from the Farm to the Pulpit

Table of Contents

Chap 1: Birth and Childhood……………………............…   1

Chap 2: Toiling On The Farm ………………….....…..   7

Chap 3: Dad Sows The Seed …………………….…….   9

Chap 4: My Schooling Begins …………………..…….. 12

Chap 5: Off To College I Go ……………………..… 14

Chap 6: Opportunities Come Knocking …………….…... 17

Chap 7: A Near-Fatal Accident …………………..… 19

Chap 8: A Life-Changing Introduction ………….........… 21

Chap 9: Debate Moderator: Bales vs Wortman ………….. 38

Chap 10: Details Of Local Work Through The Years ………. 39

Chap 11: A Door Opens For Mission Work ………….…… 43

Chap 12: The Need For Financial Support ………………. 48

Chap 13: A Few Heart-Felt Memories ……………………..…   52

Chap 14: Life Changes: Some Good - Some Not ………..…   55

Chap 15: Preacher Stories: Laughs & Tears ……................   57

Chap 16: A Few Ministry Highlights ……..………………….   65

Chap 17: "Go See My Brother" ……………………………….   71

Chap 18: My Fellow Laborers, Heroes and Hall …………...   72

*List of Preachers with Whom I Have Worked …................   72

*Heroes of the Faith – Congregations ……………………….   75

*Hall of Fame – Individuals …………...…………………….   77

Chap 19: My Last Sermon ………………………………….…   81

Chapman Family Preachers ……………………………….....   84

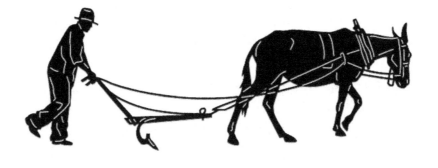

68 YEARS BEHIND THE PLOW
My Journey from the Farm to the Pulpit

Chapter 1
Birth and Childhood

On September 12, 1929 the proverbial "stork" delivered a baby boy to Adair and Elizabeth Chapman. The arrival came in their residence in Colquitt County, near Berlin, Georgia. The child was named Forrest Tyndall Chapman. Yes…..this is when I discovered America!

Forrest 6-9mos

Mother and Dad were the parents of five children — Adair, Jr. (born in 1921), Mildred (born in 1925), Forrest (born in 1929), Curtis (born in 1933) and Arlin (born in 1935). Curtis died at the age of 4 months with pneumonia. My grandfather died the next day with pneumonia, also.

**Adair Sr (Dad); Adair Jr;
Elizabeth (Mother): Arlin;
Forrest; Mildred**

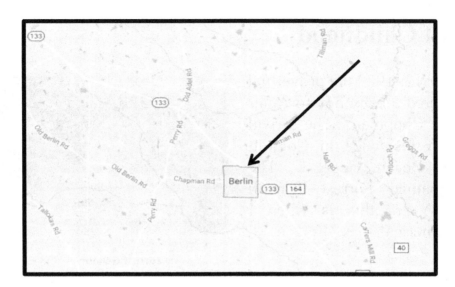

You would probably find it difficult to locate Berlin on a map. During my childhood there was an elementary school, one church, one general store, a cotton gin, the post office and - a jail! Two miles west of Berlin, on what is now Chapman Road, was the small two-horse farm where I spent 16 years.

Chapman Home – Berlin, GA

Forrest's Father and Mother

Arlin, Adair Sr., and Forrest

Forrest's Parents Celebrating Their 50th Wedding Anniversary

Forrest T. Chapman

Arlin; Mildred; Adair Sr.; Elizabeth; Forrest

Mildred **Adair Jr.** **Arlin and Forrest**

Old Barn

Forrest, Adair Jr., and Arlin

Forrest, Arlin, and Adair Jr. (at the home of Harvey Starling)

Forrest, Adair Jr., and Arlin (at the Church of Christ in Adel, GA)

Chapter 2
Toiling On The Farm

Farming in that day involved manual labor along with a mule and a plow. As children we would often work from daylight until after dark. The "money" crops were tobacco, corn, cotton, tomatoes, watermelons and vegetables. Dad believed in keeping his children involved in constructive activities. One of my chores was to milk 4 to 6 cows before going to school each day and repeating the process before going to bed.

Old Tobacco Barn

While living on the farm, a favorite memory of mine is that of Tony the Pony. Tony was a pony that Dad purchased for the children to ride. Adair Jr. was the first to ride him and eventually Tony was passed on to Mildred and then to me. Tony was previously a race pony on a racetrack near Thomasville, GA. He was always a great winner! His fame spread throughout the community. Boys would bring their horses to race against Tony. Adair Jr., Arlin and I all agree that we never lost a race. Tony was purchased in the early 30's and the purchase price was 29 hens and 3 roosters! Money was scarce in those days. Tony lived long enough for some grandchildren to ride him. One day Dad said he started to go into Moultrie and saw Tony way down in the pasture.

Adair Jr. on Tony the Pony

He whistled for him and Dad said he ran the hardest he had ever seen him run. He ran into the barn and Dad went on to town. When he returned, he went to the barn and found Tony had died. He had run his last race - but he couldn't outrun death. Neither can we in our lives. (Hebrews 9:27)

Mother was constantly busy preparing meals for the laborers and washing clothes. She cooked on a wood stove that had a side reservoir filled with water that was heated from the fire in the stove. (Similar to the one at the right.) We often used that water in a washtub for our Saturday night baths! For washing clothes there was an old iron wash pot and scrub board. Water was drawn from a nearby well. The only running water was when I would run to and from the well! We did have a "solar energy" dryer. It was called a clothesline in the sunshine. Those were the 'good ole days'.

As mentioned previously, during my childhood, most farm work was performed by manual labor - hoes, pitchforks, rakes, shovels and riding cultivators. The turning plow, pulled by a mule, was often the tool that Dad wanted me to use. Plowing usually began shortly after sunrise and continued until sunset. The pause for "dinner" was at noon. We knew it was noon when we heard the old dinner bell that was sounded by my mother. Not only did I welcome the sound but so did Cary - the mule. She would invariably stop where she was. Only after a little encouragement from me would she continue to the end of the row. It was only after I left for Harding that Dad purchased his first tractor.

**Actual Bell
Mother Rang**

Chapter 3
Dad Sows The Seed

In 1922, Dad, Mom and Jr. left the farm to attend Nashville Bible School, which is now David Lipscomb University. Some of his classmates were G.C. Brewer, Foy Wallace and B.C. Goodpasture. Having completed his studies they returned to the farm where Dad resumed his farming. By day he sowed seeds in the fields and by night he sowed the seed of the kingdom in the hearts of his neighbors and others also. Many were converted. Weekends would find him traveling to small congregations in South Georgia and North Florida to teach and lend encouragement.

Adair P Chapman Riding Off To Preach

His remuneration would be anywhere between a dime and twenty-five cents. Several congregations in South Georgia that he helped to establish and maintain are still in existence such as Adel, Hahira, Morven and Moultrie. Some of the family names I recall from some of these are Bradford, Story, Hamm, Futch, Coppage, Touchton, Shaver, Wisenbaker and Foley.

Adair P. Chapman, Sr.

Mother died in 1975 and Dad died in 1978 at the age of 89. Shortly after Mother died, Dad called and asked me if I would come and drive him to Rome, Georgia to see Uncle Bun and Aunt Myrtle. He and "Uncle Bun" had played together as children although Uncle Bun was a little older. That's why Dad called him "Uncle".

After we arrived, Dad informed him of his purpose in coming. He had come to encourage him to become a Christian. After a number of excuses and Biblical study, Dad baptized Uncle Bun and Aunt Myrtle in the bathtub! Myrtle had listened in on what Dad was teaching and said "I want to be baptized". I don't know who was happier – Dad, Bun or Myrtle. The bathtub was large enough for immersion.

Until his death, Dad was always telling others about that event! He would stop strangers on the street and say, "Let me tell you about Uncle Bun!" And he would, whether they wanted to hear it or not.

Adair P. Chapman

Chapter 4
My Schooling Begins

Berlin Elementary School was where our public education began. Transportation was provided by school buses and sometimes we had to walk a considerable distance to catch it. Dad was one of the trustees. Each day there was a devotional period with Bible reading and a short spiritual lesson. Dad was often invited to deliver the message.

At one of the school functions, there was a brief meeting of the Trustees. Some matter was being discussed that resulted in a difference of opinion. One of the trustees became so angry with Dad he wanted to fight! As he walked toward Dad to begin the physical altercation, another man quickly came between them and said, "You are not going to fight Mr. Chapman! He is my friend and if you want to fight somebody you will have to fight me first. Get out of here!" That ended the matter and the fellow turned and walked away. He later apologized for his behavior.

Forrest 15 yrs old

Forrest 17 yrs old

High school in Moultrie, some 12 miles away, was the next stop on our educational journey. Transportation was again provided by county school buses. I wanted to participate in sports but was unable to do so because farm work provided the hindrance and having to remain after school for practice made it doubly hard.

Our parents wanted us to receive a Christian education so Harding College in Searcy, Arkansas, was the selection for our higher education.

Graduating from high school, Adair was the first to go to Harding. He was soon introduced to Nancy Mullaney and she became his primary subject. So much so, when Dr. George Benson gave Adair permission to drive his automobile on college business while he was away, Adair and Nancy eloped! So, thanks to the kindness of Dr. Benson, my brother was able to get married. Mildred was the next to go to Harding and having met Kermit Ary, they began a courtship that resulted in Mildred getting her "M.R.S." degree in 1944. They were married in F.W. Maddox's living room in Searcy.

Dr. George S. Benson
Pres. of Harding College
(1936-1965)

Adair Jr. and Nancy Chapman

Chapter 5
Off To College I Go

**High School Graduation
Moultrie GA**

Then it was my time. I had been sheltered most of my life and had never been away from home to spend the night very often. Having graduated from high school in 1946, I now was excited over getting away and making the journey to Searcy, Arkansas. On a Friday morning, Dad placed my wardrobe trunk and suitcase on his truck and we drove to the Moultrie Trailways Bus Station. The trunk and suitcase were placed on the bus and after telling Dad goodbye I boarded the bus and my journey began. Several years later, I recall when Arlin left on that Trailways bus, I had gone to Moultrie with them. I was already in the truck ready to go back to the farm. Dad watched until the bus was out of sight. He turned, took out his handkerchief and wiped his eyes. That was the first time I ever saw my Dad weep. I have often wondered if he did the same when I left.

From Moultrie to Searcy was about 700 miles. Only a short time had elapsed before I had a peculiar feeling in the pit of my stomach. With every passing mile it became more and more severe. After a nine-hour layover in Birmingham, I arrived in Searcy Saturday night around midnight. By that time I had a full-blown case of homesickness!!

A cab took me to the college where someone told me the dorms were filled and I would be in a private residence with two other roommates, who turned out to be two veterans. They soon educated me in things I had never heard or read about!

However, the next year my roommate was a preacher student who was quite a contrast with my former roommates. Most students are invited to join one of the social clubs. I received the invitation to join the Koinonia Club. At the time I was unaware of it not having the best reputation. At the initiation I found evidence for that conclusion. I will only state that I survived some of the things I choose not to disclose.

Forrest (Age: 20's)

After two years, I transferred to David Lipscomb College in Nashville, TN. There I found, as a roommate, one of the finest young men I have ever met. Joe Ed Clark was also a veteran but unlike the others who were my first roommates. He was from Columbia, TN and would often take a group of us to his home for the weekend. He was always interested in spiritual matters. He was an excellent role model for all of us and was rewarded by being voted the "Bachelor of Ugliness" for the class of 1950. Joe died on January 26, 2017, after a lengthy illness in Decatur, AL.

He has told you, O man, what is good;
and what does the Lord require of you but to do justice,
and to love kindness, and to walk humbly with your God?
Micah 6:8

Chapter 6
Opportunities Come Knocking

During the summer of 1949, I went to Atlanta where I lived with Mildred and Kermit Ary - my sister and brother-in-law. I got a temporary job with Crane Plumbing Company and worshipped at East Point and West End congregations. West End invited me to speak once or twice. Upon graduating in 1950, the West End elders invited me to become the associate minister. I accepted it and many close friendships were formed that remain until this day. However after six months, I received a call from Albany, GA informing me of their need for a minister at Highland Avenue and wanted to know if I would be interested.

West End Church of Christ 1950s

The Highland Avenue congregation (now Dawson Road) had about 70 members. They knew little about me except I often, as a teenager, went with Dad and Mom where Dad preached once a month. They invited me to become their minister without a "trial" sermon! The salary was $50 per week and out of that would be $50 for room rent each month.

Dawson Road Church of Christ (Present Day)

Accepting the invitation, I arrived by Trailways Bus carrying all my earthly possessions. I had no automobile, no bank account, no experience as a minister and no wife! Courtships at Harding and Lipscomb did not produce a desirable subject for a lifetime spouse. I did not know it at the time, but the Lord was preparing the ideal mate for me and I would soon meet her!

At this time I had to depend on brethren for transportation. But it wasn't very long until one good brother sold me his 1949 Plymouth for "what you can pay and when you can pay". After three months he presented me with the title! Sister Gause, his mother, operated a boarding house with daily meals and invited me to come and eat with them anytime I desired. This helped me to keep body and soul together.

Forrest and his "new" car

Chapter 7
A Near-Fatal Accident

Shortly after that, in the winter of 1951, I was involved in a no-fault accident that demolished the 1949 Plymouth and left me bleeding profusely. This was in late January about 10PM at night and only 28 degrees. I had left church that evening to visit with my parents near Moultrie. Fortunately a "Good Samaritan" drove by and I waved to him from the side of the road. He stopped, backed up, opened the car door and gasped. "You are bleeding terribly bad – get in and I will take you to the hospital!" The hospital was 16 miles away. I got in the back seat and took off my shirt and wrapped it around my head. A few minutes later I reached down to see if there was blood on the floor. There was plenty of it and I lost consciousness. What happened after that is hearsay. I never regained consciousness until I woke up in the hospital the next morning with my face covered in bandages. I am told that when I opened the car door and tried to step out I fell to the driveway. When the driver rushed to get help, a pediatrician came along and saw where the blood was coming from and applied pressure.

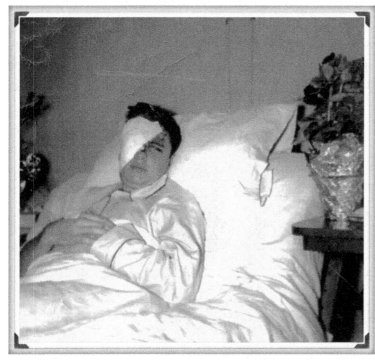
Forrest in Hospital

The doctor said five more minutes and it would have been too late. I needed a transfusion and Bro. Beasley, hearing about the accident, rushed to the hospital and had the same blood type as mine. He volunteered to give me the transfusion. He lay on the gurney next to me and I received his blood arm to arm.

I can see the providential Hand of God working in this incident. I spent five days in the hospital and two weeks recovering in the home of a lovely couple who cared for me. I was to speak at the Alabama Christian Lectureships in a few weeks and was able to keep that engagement. By that time, the good brother who sold me the 1949 Plymouth helped me purchase a new 1951 Plymouth!

Forrest in his <u>next</u> "new" car

Chapter 8
A Life-Changing Introduction

Shortly afterward, our young people invited the young people from the sister congregation to a party. There was one young lady present that I had not seen before. She was a striking brunette and as pretty as any girl I had ever seen. She was there with some young man but I introduced myself to her and she said her name was Burma. I did not think too much about it until a few weeks later. There was a gospel meeting at the sister congregation and I decided to visit. As I sat down, I looked across the aisle and there was Burma sitting next to a woman that I later learned was her aunt. I began to think perhaps this is my best opportunity to get to know her better.

Burma Wynell Yelverton

At the close of service, I stood in the aisle and she smiled when she saw me. I mustered up courage enough to say "How about me taking you home tonight?" She hesitated and then said, "Sure."

I have been taking her home for 65 years!

Forrest and Burma 'striking a pose'

We were married one year later on March 17, 1952 in Waycross, GA. Neither of us could afford an elaborate wedding so the decision was made to meet Bro. Lawrence Hazelip, who was in a meeting there, and let him perform the ceremony. We left Albany early on Monday morning and after the wedding we drove to Jacksonville, Florida where we spent our first night. Then we went on to St. Augustine, FL for Tuesday night. We left for home early Wednesday to be back for the Bible Study. Quite a honeymoon!

Mr. and Mrs. Forrest Chapman

Our Wedding

Burma with Bro. Hazelip

Forrest with Bro. Hazelip

Burma has truly been my soul mate, helpmeet and willing to quietly go about doing anything and everything expected of a preacher's wife. If we contemplated a move, she would be agreeable with the attitude of Ruth, "Whither thou goest, I will go." Our love for each other has never died; but a few times it's been a little "feverish"!!

Forrest and Burma

We have three children, Forrest Tyndall, Jr. born in Albany, GA, Katrina Cay born in Valdosta, GA, and Loren Thomas was born in Atlanta, GA.

Burma, Tyndall and Forrest

Burma and Cay

Burma and Tommy

All three graduated from Greater Atlanta Christian School and all three played on State Championship basketball teams at GACS.

Tommy, Cay, Burma, Forrest, and Tyndall

Our children never presented us with major problems. To my knowledge they never smoked, drank alcohol or got involved with drugs. Being in GACS in that day made the difference. Tyndall was considered a "superstar" in basketball, scoring 56 points in one game against a rival team. That record still stands.

Forrest Chapman Family

Tommy, Cay, and Tyndall

Tommy and Cay   **Tommy**   **Cay and Tyndall**

Forrest T. Chapman

Forrest Chapman Family

Tyndall, Forrest, Tommy, Burma and Cay

Forrest Chapman Family

Tommy

Cay, Forrest and Tyndall

Cay and Forrest

Forrest T. Chapman

Father & Sons Roundup Dinner

Tommy, Forrest and Tyndall

Our children have presented us with seven grandchildren and five great-grandchildren!

GRANDKIDS - THEN

Maggie; Brian; Tyler (being held); Lesley; Julie

GRANDKIDS - NOW

Lesley and Maggie (Tyndall's Kids)

Julie, Tyler and Brian (Cay's Kids)

Mallory and Michele (Tommy's Kids)

GREAT-GRANDKIDS
(with MawMaw & PawPaw)

Carter, MawMaw, MaCayla, PawPaw, Annistyn and Hudson
(Adaline was not born when the above picture was taken)

Adaline (Born Dec. 24 2017)

FOUR GENERATIONS!

Burma, Julie, and Cay
Adaline and Annistyn

Chapter 9
Debate Moderator: Bales vs Wortman

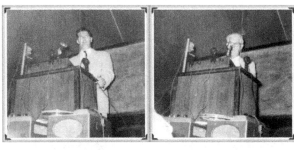

James D. Bales   **Mr. Wortman**

An atheist by the name of Wortman was quite vocal in his denial of the existence of God. He frequently wrote articles in the paper challenging anyone to debate the issue with him. Bro. James D. Bales had debated a champion of atheism, Woolsey Teller, at Harding College. Bro. Bales soundly defeated him! (That debate is in print.) I called Bro. Bales and made arrangements for him to get in touch with Mr. Wortman. A debate was arranged and scheduled with Mr. Wortman. It was conducted under a tent near the church building. The bottom line is that Bro. Bales defeated him soundly. It was obvious because Mr. Wortman never replied or rebutted any of Bro. Bales' arguments. Instead, he read from prepared manuscripts. Mr. Wortman was not quite as vocal after that. It was an honor for me to serve as moderator.

Forrest and James D. Bales

Forrest (as Debate Moderator)

Chapter 10
Details of My Local Work Through the Years

My first local work was at Highland Avenue (now Dawson Road) in Albany, GA for three years. From there we moved to Valdosta and I preached at the River Street congregation for three years which is now known as Forrest Park. Next, we moved to North Avenue in Hapeville, GA, a suburb of Atlanta and stayed there for eight years. An invitation to move to Daytona Beach, FL to work with the Bay Street congregation was accepted with some reluctance. However, this was the most fruitful work I have ever had. The congregation outgrew the building on Bay Street and purchased property on Beville Road.

Bay Street Member (Daytona Beach) Welcomes Forrest and His Family

Constant Bible studies were being conducted and we had many baptisms. I have never been associated with any brethren who were more loving, caring and gracious than those in Daytona. Our children were growing up and the atmosphere was not conducive for rearing children to my way of thinking. Thus, we made the difficult decision to move back to Georgia. The invitation came from Forrest Park in Valdosta, where we had previously worked. The new building in Daytona was completed and I preached the first sermon in it on Sunday and moved on Monday. We had been there for two years. After spending two years in Valdosta, we had an invitation to return to North Avenue in Hapeville, GA. It was accepted and we returned to work with them for 16 years before entering the Georgia Mission Field.

Forrest at North Avenue

North Avenue – Hapeville GA

A Close Call. Upon our arrival in Daytona Beach we were greeted by three hurricanes in a row. High winds and heavy rain pelted the area where we lived but no serious damage was done. A friend invited me to go with him to the beach side to see what was taking place there. He drove a truck with a camper attached. Tyndall, our oldest son, asked to go along and ride in the back. With the weather like it was, I insisted that he ride up front with us. After we were driving along Front Beach, a sudden surge of wind struck us and the camper was torn from the back of the truck. My insistence that Tyndall ride up front turned out to be a wise decision.

Our Return. Going back to North Avenue where we had worked previously for eight years, was like going back home. It seems the entire congregation was pleased with the decision. Attendance began to increase and baptisms were frequent and others were restored, while some placed membership with us. Soon the attendance surpassed 300. The balcony was often filled to capacity and the elders formulated plans for a new building. Two lots next door were purchased for the erection of the building and also additional parking. All of this had come after assisting some brethren to begin congregations in Forest Park and Riverdale. The Lord was "giving the increase". The fellowships we enjoyed provided a continuation of unity, participation and enthusiasm.

**Forrest at North Ave
Hapeville GA**

Greater Atlanta Christian Schools had been established in Norcross, GA and our children, along with others, took advantage of transportation and enrolled. Our dream in Florida for our children to have a Christian education had come true. All three of our children graduated from GACS and all three played on State Championship basketball teams there. I even had three of my grandchildren to attend for a while as well as a son-in-law who served as a teacher for 26 years with GACS.

Groundbreaking for GACS – 1960s

During these years at North Avenue there were many births and many deaths. We rejoiced with the births and wept at the deaths. A major blow was the loss of Bro. Claude Taylor and Bro. Winford Lentz - elders at the North Avenue congregation.

CHAPTER 11
A Door Opens for Mission Work

Entering the mission work was truly a challenge and blessing. This brought me in contact with countless people whom we regard as 'salt-of-the-earth'. Friendships and fellowships were established with brethren all over the state of Georgia and other states as well. My work with these small rural congregations brought me much enjoyment as I assisted and encouraged them along the way.

What a thrill it was to introduce people to simple New Testament Christianity. Many had never realized they could simply be Christians only without human names and adherence to creeds written by men. The Bible only still makes Christians only. We began with campaigns, the printed page and radio. At one time we had seventeen radio broadcasts around the state in rural areas. Many were timed to follow Paul Harvey (a popular newscaster) and the local news.

I had encouraged my good friend and brother in Christ, Bob Gray, to also get involved. He was preaching at East Point but he resigned and soon was involved with Georgia Mission work with his lovely, dedicated wife, Betty. They have accomplished more in the state of Georgia than any others. We have enjoyed many hours of pleasant association with them.

Prior to entering the Georgia Mission Field, evangelistic work was the result of invitations to conduct gospel meetings. Some of these were in Georgia, Florida, Alabama, Louisiana, Mississippi, Arkansas, Kentucky, Kansas and Texas.

Memorable meetings were conducted in Reedyville, Kentucky. The little congregation was called Bethlehem. It was located about 25 miles from Bowling Green. My first meeting there was in the mid-50's. Conditions were rather primitive. Roads were unpaved and rivers were crossed by ferry as the picture to the right illustrates. Few houses had electricity and outdoor "facilities" were common. The little church building consisted of no classrooms and open windows provided the ventilation. Animals would frequently visit the services! One night while I  was there, a barking dog came running in. Someone quickly used his foot to get him out! Above the pulpit was a bell. The rope to ring the bell for time to begin the service hung just above the preacher's head and it was tied similar to a noose!

I believed that served as a warning for the preacher!

"Moonshining" and "Bootlegging" were still prevalent in that community. Revenue agents often raided the "stills", destroyed them and arrested those involved like the picture to the right. To my knowledge, I never met a "bootlegger" while I was there. Some could've been present as I preached or possibly even members of the congregation!

Some years before I had arrived there a Gospel preacher was delivering his sermon when he was shot and killed! Rumors had circulated that he was a revenue agent. His wife was not injured. Needless to say, I chose my sermon topics with great care!

Through the years one man had attended with regularity. His wife was a faithful member but Fred showed little interest in having a personal Bible study. One year I returned and Fred was still present for each service. I asked Rodney, with whom we were staying, to go with me to visit Fred.

He greeted us cordially and after a few minutes I said, "Fred, you have been so faithful in attending the service and I want to ask you a question. (Fred was now 79.) Have you ever thought about obeying the gospel?" His answer surprised me. "I think about it all the time". Then I said, "At 79, don't you think you need to stop thinking about it and do something about it?" He replied, "It is; and I want to be baptized." We took him and baptized him that afternoon. There was great joy in the congregation when the announcement was made that evening.

A year later I was back for another meeting and asked Rodney how Fred was getting along. He said "Forrest, I thought you knew. Fred died about six months after you were here." I was so thankful that Rodney and I had made that visit the year before.

I was back there a few years later and conditions had drastically changed. Oil had been found in that community and many changes had occurred --- roads were paved, bridges were over rivers, there were tractors instead of mules, and brick homes were evident with air conditioning. The church building had been refurbished with new flooring and air conditioning. There was even indoor plumbing for men and women! There was a baptistery now and so we no longer had to use the river for baptizing converts similar to the picture below.

Baptism in Monroe Co, KY

We were fortunate to lodge for several years with Rodney and Edith Gary who had a lovely home with facilities that others did not have. Rodney raised corn and was also in the hog business. Edith was a school teacher. They, along with the majority we met, were truly 'salt-of-the-earth'. Rodney had to be placed in a special facility after developing Alzheimer's. Edith sold the farm and moved into Bowling Green to be close and cared for him until he passed away.

We were through Bowling Green a few years ago and spent the night with her. Edith said he hardly recognized her anymore and seldom said anything. We visited with him the next day and she said he would probably not say anything. I spoke to him and said, "Rodney, do you remember a preacher by the name of Chapman who held meetings at Bethlehem and stayed with you and Edith?" He looked at me and said, "Chapman – Forrest Chapman?" Edith looked at me and laughed. "I never thought he would answer you!" Edith still lives but Rodney died about three or so years ago. These were some very 'precious memories'!

Chapter 12
The Need for Financial Support

Getting started and continuing the work was dependent on financial support. Without the support of individuals and congregations we could not have survived for very long. Every missionary, local or foreign, realizes the necessity of financial support. Recognizing this, there was much prayer that financial support would be supplied for me. "With much fear and trembling", I resigned local work and walked by faith and not by sight.

My first visit was to Dawson Road in Albany. I relayed to the elders my plans for Georgia Evangelism, taking the gospel to places that had been neglected. They were excited over my plans and immediately decided they wanted to be involved. They made a substantial first month's support and continued some support until I had to terminate my work for health issues.

Bobby Terrell, a good friend and fellow preacher, was preaching for Walnut Street in Dickson, TN. He made plans for me to visit one weekend and lay my plans before the elders. I was delighted when they agreed to be a major contributor for an indefinite period of time. Their support continued until June of last year (2017), which was over twenty-five years! They have truly been loyal and faithful brethren!

Many congregations have helped to some degree through the years. These include: Hillsboro, TN; North Avenue – Hapeville, GA; Fayetteville, GA; Gordon, GA; McCaysville, GA; Mt. Olive, TN; Hiawassee, GA; Beville Road, FL; North Macon, GA; Savannah, GA; and Shurlington, GA.

SOME PLACES WHERE I HAVE HELD CAMPAIGNS & GOSPEL MEETINGS THROUGH THE YEARS

Adel GA   Hayesville NC

Barnesville GA
(Workers from Fayetteville Congregation)

SOME PLACES WHERE I HAVE HELD CAMPAIGNS & GOSPEL MEETINGS THROUGH THE YEARS

Gordon GA

Lakeland GA

Newcastle IN

Waynesboro GA

SOME PLACES WHERE I HAVE HELD CAMPAIGNS & GOSPEL MEETINGS THROUGH THE YEARS

Manchester GA

Chapter 13
Some Special Memories

Burma and I spent a total of 24 years at North Avenue in Hapeville, GA. During that time we enjoyed a pleasant relationship without any disturbance of unity. Within those years I performed numerous weddings and later baptized and married their children. We rejoiced at the birth of children and wept at the passing of loved ones. Through the 24 years I conducted over 250 funerals and baptized several hundred. Once again, "God gives the increase!"

One Sunday a young couple attended services. I met them and obtained their address which was near the church building. After visiting with them and showing them a series of filmstrips by Jule Miller, they were baptized and became very active in the congregation. David and Melva Kodatt became dear friends of ours. He went on to serve as an elder. At retirement, they moved to Hiawassee, GA and we soon followed them and spent much time together up in the mountains. They have both gone to their reward but the memories linger.

"Parson's Perch"

**Forrest and Burma
North Georgia Mountain Home
Hiawassee, GA**

JJ and Isabele Turner

A young couple came to church one Sunday as a result of a co-worker asking him to visit North Avenue. We got acquainted and visited with them, and also showed them the Jule Miller filmstrips. They were baptized and immediately became involved in all of our activities. His interest peaked and suggested to me his desire to attend a preacher training school. The only one at that time was Sunset School of Preaching in Lubbock, Texas. I helped to raise funds for them and they moved to Lubbock.

After graduating from Sunset he furthered his education and has become one of the most respected and well-known preachers in our brotherhood both as a preacher and author. Who is it? It is my good friend and brother in the Lord, J.J. Turner and his wife, Isabele. J.J. is now preacher and elder at McDonough Church of Christ and was the Founding President of the World Bible Institute. He presently serves as the school's Chancellor located at the McDonough church site. If you haven't read some of his books, you should!

On another Sunday, a couple from a few blocks away attended the service. Their daughter, Barbara, was already a member. The following week I visited their home. The lady, answering my knock, was surprised to see a preacher coming unannounced. She cordially invited me in and that visit resulted in their coming back to services.

The two of them were baptized a few weeks later. A close friendship with Cliff and Sue Bramlett was formed and we have enjoyed the relationship for 60 years.

Sue recently observed her 95th birthday and we were pleased to attend and share the joy of that occasion at the McDonough Church of Christ where she is a member.

Their decision also resulted in the conversion of her brother and his wife, Rufus and Lettie Huff, as well as their invalid son who was also baptized. Through the years we have shared many joys and sorrows with these families.

Sue (Bramlett) Johnson and Forrest

Chapter **14**
Life Changes: Some Good – Some Not

I began Georgia Mission work in 1982. This necessitated our moving out of the "parsonage". Fortunately, we purchased a house directly behind the church building at North Avenue in Hapeville, GA. It had previously been the home of Claude and Tinie Taylor. Bro. Taylor served as an elder at North Avenue for many years. Burma had been employed with Delta Airlines for several years and this location enabled her to travel the same distance each day to work.

In 1988 I was diagnosed with prostate cancer. Treatments consisted of radiation beams over a period of weeks. These left me in a weakened condition but the cancer became dormant. I was able to resume my schedule after a few weeks.

In 1991 Burma retired from Delta and we made the decision to move to Hiawassee, GA. This location was in the heart of a "mission field". We could work with the small congregation and still continue to assist others such as Hayesville and Cornelia. During this time I did interim works with the good congregations in Woodstock and Savannah. The Bull Street congregation in Savannah had some internal problems that resulted in the sale of the beautiful historical building with members scattering in different directions. My interim work was with the group now known as the Central church.

In 2000 the cancer returned and I underwent surgery for the implanting of radiation seeds. This has been effective and no cancer now exists. However, my current problems are traced to the radiation. Scar tissue has caused bladder and other problems for which there has been no cure. One experimental drug has affected my vocal cords resulting in the termination of my work. There also remains a great amount of discomfort.

For 68 years I have been "behind the plow". I have preached for churches of Christ in 16 states and 3 foreign countries. But now it has been laid aside as I await the day when "all things will be made new." Rev. 21:5. My sentiment is that of the apostle Paul in 2 Tim 4 ……..

"I have fought a good fight.
I have finished my course.
I have kept the faith….."
2 Tim 4:7

Chapter 15
Preacher Stories: Laughs & Tears
Laughter

During my 68 years in the ministry, as it is with most ministers, there is a mixture of joy and sorrow. Some examples of both follow:

A MISUNDERSTANDING
One Sunday at North Avenue I had just begun my sermon when a lady cried out from the back of the auditorium, "Help Me!" There was quite a commotion and the service disturbed. I quickly said to the song leader, "Barney, lead a song while they minister to the lady." Well, Barney must have been unaware of what was happening and thought I meant for him to lead the invitation song and so he began – "Come to Jesus Dying Sinner!" There was an eruption of laughter and then things quieted down as the service continued – and thankfully, the lady survived!

Stanley Johnson, Forrest, and Barney Sullivan (Song Leader at North Ave)

WATCH YOUR STEP
A lady who had recently placed membership at North Avenue volunteered to prepare the communion. She was informed that she would find all the necessary items in the kitchen and it was usually prepared on Saturday. After keeping her appointment with her hairdresser on Saturday, she came to the entrance of the basement where I had unlocked the door. About 15 minutes later she came out and drove off, only to return a few minutes later. I had viewed all of this from the den where I was sitting across the street.

Such activity aroused my curiosity and I walked over. As I entered I saw no lights were on. No one had informed her that there was a master switch that controlled all the lights in the building. I hit the light switch and called to her. She answered from down the hallway and asked me not to come around there. I couldn't resist. What I saw was really indescribable!

I saw her standing in the doorway of the kitchen with communion trays sitting on the stove and she was trying to fill the cups out of the bottle. Grape juice was everywhere! Then I looked at her and she looked as though *she* had been baptized! She was wet all over! Her hair was wet and her pantsuit seemed already to be shrinking. There was a puddle of water at her feet. She proceeded to explain what had happened.

Upon entering the building and since she could not find the light switch she began to search for the kitchen. Opening one door she saw a stairway leading upward and when she reached the top there was a door that led only to the auditorium. The stairway continued upward and she assumed that would lead to the kitchen. She reached the top and saw, in the semi-darkness, a dressing room. After taking only a few steps she found herself in the baptistery!! Her purse contents and a bottle of grape juice were "baptized"! She went up the other side only to find another dressing room. She decided against going down the other stairway and instead walked back through the baptistery. She exited the building and drove off to the corner store to get more grape juice!

I assisted her in preparing the communion and she asked me never to tell anybody about what had happened. I made no promise because it was too good to keep! Fortunately, she was not injured and I have never found a better example of pure determination!

I QUIT WHEN I WAS EIGHT YEARS OLD

My big brother, Adair Jr., was known as Junior before leaving home. Being eight years younger I regarded him as my hero and capable of doing most anything. He was strong and muscular - a "Charles Atlas" to me. There were several things he taught me: how to ride Tony the Pony, how to make a sling shot, how to swim, and how to shoot the guns that belonged to Dad.

When Junior was 17 years old he asked mother if she would let him and three friends go fishing in a creek that was about half a mile from our house through a wooded area. Normally, he would have had to ask Dad to go but he was not available. So he asked mother instead. She said, "Yes, but only if you let Forrest go with you". He reluctantly agreed. Arriving at the fishing hole I realized they had no fishing equipment and had no intention of fishing. Instead they had a sack full of cigars. Instead of fishing they wanted to smoke those cigars and Junior swore me to secrecy. After they began, I decided I also would like to have one of those cigars. Junior said, "Alright, but don't tell Daddy."

Shortly after I began to smoke, an unpleasant feeling came over me. The longer I smoked the longer that cigar became! Suddenly I was overcome by nausea and dizziness. I became so sick that I could not stand up. Naturally, this alarmed Junior. He had not anticipated it affecting me that way. He picked me up and literally carried me all the way home. I suppose that was his punishment. Mother was concerned when she saw me lying in the front porch swing and asked Junior what had happened to me. He told her the whole story but asked that she not tell Daddy. I do not know if she did or not but Dad never mentioned it to me and I was certainly not about to bring it up.

This experience was a blessing in disguise because I have never had the desire to smoke after that. When Doctors have asked me if I smoke, I answer by saying, "I quit when I was eight years old"!!

I truly believe that preachers who smoke, not only harm their bodies but their influence as God's servant (I Cor. 6:20).

"For ye are bought with a price: therefore glorify God in your body, and in your spirit, which are God's."

Preacher Stories: Laughs & Tears
Tears

A FALLEN BROTHER

Preachers must often gather with friends who have lost a loved one. For me during the 68 years, I have conducted well over 500 funerals. Among those I  will share two of the saddest. A young man at North Avenue was in the military. Shortly after marriage he was deployed to Vietnam. Before he left, he talked with me about his fears and his faith. After being in Vietnam only a few weeks, word came to his family that he had been killed. We can only imagine the sorrow that invaded the hearts of that family. Adding to the stress was the length of time it required to return the remains. When the time came the request was made for Mike Johnson, another young military man from North Avenue, to escort the body. The request was granted and Mike stood tall as he spent many hours serving in that capacity. Lamar Howell, Jr. paid the supreme sacrifice and we honor his memory. Lamar's name is inscribed on the Vietnam Veterans Memorial Wall on Panel 31W, Line 5.

CALVIN LAMAR HOWELL JR
PFC - E2 - Marine Corps
Birth: Sept 17, 1948
Tour began: Jan 7, 1969
Casualty on: Feb 23, 1969
In QUANG NAM, SOUTH VIETNAM
HOSTILE, GROUND CASUALTY
GUN, SMALL ARMS FIRE
http://thewall-usa.com/info

A HORRIBLE FAMILY TRAGEDY

The other saddest funeral was in Albany, Ga. When I preached there, Burma and I often double dated with a lovely couple that were engaged to be married – Ida Mae Hayes and C.D. Ranew. They asked me to perform their wedding. It was my first wedding ceremony and it was a beautiful garden wedding. Later, Burma and I were married and we continued a close relationship with Ida and C.D. Ranew.

C.D. and Ida Mae Ranew & Forrest

The years passed and we had moved away but would see them on visits to Albany. They had a family by then with grown children and we did as well. I was conducting a meeting there in October 1988. At the close of the service C.D. asked me when we could come visit them. I promised that after the first of the year we would set a time for a visit.

In late January 1989, one Sunday morning, I received a phone call from Jim Shadwick, their preacher, saying he had some bad news. The news was that Ida, C.D. and a 20 year-old daughter, Laura, had been brutally murdered. The family had asked him to call me to see if I would come conduct the funerals. Without knowing whether I could emotionally be prepared to do so, I agreed to come.

When I arrived I learned their 18 year-old son, Clay, had taken their lives in such a brutal manner. He was high on drugs. I remembered C.D. telling me he was concerned that his son was on drugs. He often asked him for money that C.D. would not give him.

Little did C.D. know just how involved he was and what the future would reveal. Over 1000 people attended the service and I struggled to find words that would somehow comfort them. The son was present, handcuffed between two detectives, but showed no signs of remorse or grief as he laid a rose on each casket. He remains in prison serving a life sentence. Among Ida Mae's survivors were six sisters. The oldest one lived in Americus and through the years when I would be speaking at Dawson Road, she would make her plans to be there. I have lost touch with the others and she recently passed away.

Gravesite for C.D., Ida Mae and Laura Ranew

THE BUTTERMILK PREACHER

During my first local work in Valdosta we established a close relationship with many of the brethren. The O'Neal family was among them. Charles and Gladys operated a dairy and distributed milk to customers in Lowndes County. Charles soon learned that I loved buttermilk, and kept me well supplied!

In visits to Valdosta, after we had moved, he would have buttermilk waiting for me. He called me his "Buttermilk Preacher". Upon one visit we learned that he was in a nursing home and at the point of death. Burma and I rushed over to find all the family had gathered to be with him. They informed me that apparently, he was in a coma because he had not opened his eyes or said anything all day. I walked over by the side of his bed and took his hand in mine. I said, "Charles, this is your 'buttermilk preacher' and if you understand, just squeeze my hand." To the astonishment of his family, he squeezed my hand harder than he ever had before! I spoke a few words to him and had a prayer with him as well as his family. We left and shortly after he passed away.

Charles O'Neal

Each time I drink buttermilk today, I remember Charles. Precious Memories.

Chapter 16
A Few Ministry Highlights

There are so many events that stand out as reflections are made on my life. However, here are just a few I wish to highlight.

TRIP TO THE 'HOLY LANDS'
There were visits made to the Holy Land on two separate occasions. Brother Ken Golson and I were able to make the trip at a reduced rate offered to Delta employees. Since Burma worked with Delta I was qualified. We flew to New York, spent the night and flew to Tel Aviv the next morning. It was fascinating to see the sun come up at 2am.

Forrest at Sea of Galilee

Seeing places where Jesus taught, walked and was crucified created a special feeling within my heart. There is nothing "Holy" about the land but this realization makes it special.

Forrest at Masada

A second visit with Burma and a group from Douglasville enabled us to visit additional places not made on the first trip. The Jordan River, the Dead Sea, Mount of Olives, Garden of Gethsemane, Masada, Mt. Carmel and Sea of Galilee were all places of great interest. At night I would read the scriptures pertaining to those places where we had gone which further enlightened my study.

Masada - Fortress of Herod the Great

CAMPAIGN TO ROMANIA

A Romanian visit was made with a campaign by Harvey Starling. Romania is part of East-Central Europe and borders the Black Sea. It's east of Italy and northwest of Turkey. It was like stepping back in time. Primitive conditions prevailed everywhere. Parcels of land, rented by others for farming, were prevalent. Manual labor was used to plant, cultivate and harvest. Few tractors were visible. Opportunities to teach and study with prospects were found on every hand but we had to do so through an interpreter. One young man in particular showed much interest. He served as our interpreter and was baptized. However, it seemed his desire was to come to America. He was told he would need a sponsor for financial support. This never materialized.

Forrest Conducting A Bible Study in Romania

Forrest with New Sister in Christ

CAMPAIGN TO ISLAND OF TRINIDAD

Another highlight was a campaign with Harvey Starling and others to the tiny island of Trinidad off the northeastern coast of Venezuela. Never had I seen such a fervent desire on the part of people to study the Bible. Requests for studies were more than we could fulfill. Brother Russell Black and I studied with two sisters who operated a boarding house. They had known nothing but Catholicism. They used their Bibles to follow along as we studied. One passage was Romans 6: 3-4:

Harvey Starling

3 Or do you not know that as many of us as were baptized into Christ Jesus were baptized into His death? 4 Therefore we were buried with Him through baptism into death, that just as Christ was raised from the dead by the glory of the Father, even so we also should walk in newness of life. (NKJV)

They asked us to reread it several times. They looked at one another and said, "We haven't been baptized. Will you baptize us?" They realized baptism is immersion. They wanted to be baptized as soon as possible. After their baptism, we studied more with them as to what Christians are to do.

Before leaving there, they prepared a dinner for us as well as others in the campaign. Conditions for eating were not the best but we managed to do so without offending them. We were very thankful for their gracious hospitality.

I have often wondered what happened to them after we departed. The church was established and I hope follow up was done for them and others that were baptized while we were there.

Forrest with old-school "power-point"
(Lesson written on a linen sheet with graphics)

THE POLLARD FAMILY & A SPECIAL HONOR

At North Avenue, there was the Pollard family. Most of them were faithful and I was always impressed with the knowledge Bro. Paul Pollard had of the scripture and secular topics also. One son, Paul Jr., went to Harding and ultimately became a professor in the Bible and languages department. He continued to do graduate work in England. Paul suggested my name to the committee selecting those who would be honored with the Distinguished Service Award in 2006. They selected me and it was quite an honor to have the presentation during the Lectureship at the college!

**Forrest Receiving Distinguished Service Award
Harding University**

Chapter **17**
"Go See My Brother"

Shortly after beginning Georgia Mission work, I visited East Point to inform the congregation of my desire to reach many who had never heard of "Restoring New Testament Christianity." The suggestion was made for anyone who had friends or relatives that might appreciate a visit to let me know and I would do my best to visit them.

A lovely lady approached me afterward and asked if I knew where Lenox, GA was located. I said, "Yes, I pass that way each time I go to Valdosta." She asked, "Will you go see my brother? He and his wife are so confused they don't know which way to turn religiously." I promised her I would.

Within the next 10 days, I was knocking on their door. Edgar operated a barber shop on his property. He closed the door and put a sign up that he would return soon. I went in and met his wife and for three hours we studied and answered questions. The Bible answered their questions.

They subsequently were baptized into Christ. The Sneads are Christians only today because of Georgia Mission work and a sister who said: "Will you go see my brother?" The sister was Sadie Moreland. She, along with her sister, Theresa Green, are both members at Fayetteville Church of Christ.

Perhaps you have a brother, sister, friend – someone is ready to go. Just ask.

Chapter 18
My Fellow Laborers;
Heroes of the Faith & Hall of Fame

~List of Preachers with Whom I Have Worked~

During the 68 years of my ministry I have been associated with and worked with many preachers. This list is not complete but these come to mind.

Kermit Ary – GA (my brother-in-law)

Terry Broome – GA & AL

Bob Bryson – Valdosta, GA – Forrest Park

Adair & Arlin Chapman – GA, Texas, Kansas, Indiana (my brothers)

Clyde Chatman – Macon area – Motivated me to do Ga Mission work

Clarence DeLoach – TN

H.A. Fincher – GA; Preacher and Bible Department Chair of GACS

Harry Goff – Macon Area

Joe Goodspeed – Valdosta 60 years ago

Bob Gray – 50 year co-worker in GA; First worked together to establish church in Lakeland, GA

Richard & Scott Harp – Atlanta area

Faron Hamner – Albany, GA

~List of Preachers with Whom I Have Worked~

Tom Harrison – TN & GA

Lawrence Hazelip (he performed our wedding ceremony) worked in GA meetings

Woodrow Hazelip – TN

Billy Helms – Ga & AL

Malcomb Hill – Forest Park, GA over 50 years ago

John Klimko – GA

Bill Long – In GA & Kentucky over 50 years ago

William Lybrand – GA & AL

Roger MacKenzie – Atlanta area

John Massey – GA – started Lavonia church with him

Evans McMullen – 60 years as co-workers in many GA mission points. Evans and his wife, Lenora, have done more to further the cause of Christ in South Georgia than any couple I know.

Gary Pollard – Hiawassee & South GA

Paul Pollard – Arkansas – Suggested me for Distinguished Servant Award given at Harding lectureship in 2006

Keith Ritchie – MaCaysville, Ga

Clifford Rumley – Hapeville, GA – Great encourager

Forrest T. Chapman

~List of Preachers with Whom I Have Worked~

Glen Schliebner – Gordon, Gray, Milledgeville – Always a joy to be with him

Harvey Starling – worked with him in Trinidad, Romania, and GA

Gentry Stults – GA & FL

Bobby Terrell – Ga, Tenn, and Illinois – introduced me to Dickson, TN elders

J.J. Turner – GA; Preacher at McDonough Church of Christ

Jere Via – GA - He was invaluable to Hiawassee after my illness

Charles White – GA

Jeff Wilder – GA

Charles Williams – GA & TN

*ALL of these at some time in my life have given me much encouragement.

HEROES of the FAITH
~ Congregations ~

Within these <u>supporting</u> congregations, you will find some that I consider to be **Heroes of the Faith**. No doubt, many have been overlooked but not intentionally. Some are deceased but deserve a place in my **Hall of Fame**. I begin with the first ones involved:

<u>Dawson Road, Albany, GA</u> – George Howell, one of the elders was excited over being partners with me and promised a substantial amount that continued until 2016. Members that also gave much encouragement were Phelps & Louise Mallard; Tommy & Florence Gurr; Terry and Murlene Jones as well as the Hicks, Lewis, Harrold, and Parrish families.

<u>Walnut Street, Dickson, TN</u> – Dan Erranton & the elders. This good church gave substantial support to our work in Hiawassee for 25 years.

<u>Mount Olive, Cumberland Furnace, TN</u> – King & Sara Welker, Bobby & Millie Denton – elders. This small congregation has given for many years and now gives benevolent support.

<u>Hillsboro, TN</u> – Kenneth Winnett and elders. This small congregation was encouraging to me when I was a student at David Lipscomb College and continued support until 2017. Through the years we made our home with Kenneth and Nell Winnett when we went there for meetings.

<u>McCaysville, GA</u> – A small congregation in North Georgia. Support has continued during my illness due mainly to Ken & Charlene Johnson's influence. A fine congregation and very mission minded.

Forrest T. Chapman

HEROES of the FAITH
~ Congregations ~

North Macon, GA – I have preached at most congregations in the Macon area over a period of 60 years. When I wrestled with the decision to enter the Georgia Mission field, my good friend and fellow preacher, Clyde Chatman gave me counsel and encouragement to do so. Shurlington, where he preached, began financial support and when Shurlington disbanded most members went to North Macon and the good congregation continues their support. Jimmy Chatman, along with Reggie Osbon, are both elders of the congregation.

Gordon, Georgia – This was one of my first mission points. For 13 consecutive years we enjoyed campaigns, meetings and other good works. Glen Schliebner was the preacher most of these years and John Hardy, Kenneth Minter and Chip Grinstead now carry on the work.

Fayetteville, Georgia – The fine congregation in Fayetteville has given me much encouragement. My association with Fayetteville spans a period of 50+ years. Their support financially has continued "in appreciation for the work I have done for 68 years." Also when my condition does not permit my presence at the services we can, through the Internet, continue our worship. We can attend on most Sunday mornings the Bible Study class and worship but seldom the evening services due to medical procedures that are necessary but can participate by means of the Internet. This church is blessed with a capable, compassionate eldership in Jim Garner, Tom Durden, Greg Nash and Jim Pelfrey. They also have deacons and teachers who faithfully serve as well as having an excellent preacher in Dave Rogers and an energetic youth minister in David Gulledge.

Beville Road, FL, Forest Park Valdosta, GA, Cedar Grove, GA, North Ave, Hapeville, GA -
All these congregations have made financial contributions along the way.

68 Years Behind The Plow

HALL of FAME
~ Individuals ~

From the beginning of my ministry I recall many individuals who have given me much encouragement and assistance at some phase of my 68 year ministry. I feel that these should be in my "**Hall of Fame**". It would require another book if I told why each one is so special to me. I know I have left out names that were also very important to me but please know it was not intentional! Special thanks and memories to:

Tommy & Susan Arnold; Kermit & Mildred Ary; Ashley & Paula Ary; Ted Ary; Franklin & Sabrina Bailey; Jeff & Ruby Bailey; Ronald & Jerry Bailey; Lester Beasley & wife; Ronnie & Judy Beckwith; Louise Benefield; Russell and Floyce Black; Jackie Bradford*; Cliff, Sue & Barbara Bramlett; Bob & Kate Bryant; Roy Carroll; Clay & Het Cates; Harry Cauble; Clyde, Jimmy, Evelyn, Debbie & Kim Chatman; Glen & Virginia Cochran; Ray & Barbara Cozart; Bobby & Millie Denton; Walt & Urenda Driver; Jim & Anna Mae Duren;

Dennis & Marlene Ethridge; Jeff and Martha Fagan; Louie & Betty Flythe; Ed & Kathleen Garner; Jim & Sandy Garner; A.C. & Mildred Gibson; Bob & Betty Gray; Tommy & Florence Gurr; Tom Harrison; Billy & Norma Helms; Loge & Norma Hesson; Lewis & Kathy Hicks; Pete Howell; Curtis & Jo Hurt; Tony & Gennine Jarman; Robert & Shirley Jarrard; Stanley, Louise, Mike & Loujean Johnson; Ken & Charlene Johnson; Terry & Murlene Jones;

Hugh & Connie Kelly; John Kilmko; Dave & Melva Kodatt; Jack Kyle; Harold & Virginia Lee; Bill Long; Ann Mallard; Phelps & Louise Mallard; J. B & Alice Martin; Mike McCullough; Evans & Lenora McMullen; Joe & Janice Moody; Austin & Gladys Moore; Shep & Betty Moss; Wayne & Betty Jo Nash; Greg & Amy Nash; Charles & Gladys O'Neal; Sammy Polk; Jake & Dorothy Parker; Josephine Paul; Bo & Linda Powell; C.J. & Memphis Roberts; Clyde & Ruth Roberts; Glen & Phyllis Schliebner; Barney & Margaret Sullivan;

Forrest T. Chapman

HALL of FAME
~ Individuals ~

C.C. & Tinie Taylor; Bobby & Barbara Terrell; Bill & Jean Turner; J.J. & Isabele Turner; Versie & Mary Valentine; Jere & Sue Via; Louis & Martha Vickery; Herbert Watkins; King & Sara Welker; Sue West; Eula White; Charles & Elaine Whitmire; Jack & Spuz Williams; Faye Wilson; Emelle & Leta Woodham; and Leonard Wright.

*A special appreciation to Jackie Bradford for planning and preparing a birthday/appreciation luncheon for me in September 2017. Members of my family and mostly preachers were in attendance. Jackie served as basketball coach at GACS in the early years and coached Tyndall and Tommy. I knew Jackie's parents and enjoyed their hospitality on several occasions.

Family and Preacher Friends Celebrate with Forrest His 88th Birthday

LAST BUT NOT LEAST – MY PRECIOUS FAMILY!

Burma, My Beloved Wife

My children and their spouses - Tyndall & Mandy Chapman; Mike & Cay Adams; and Tommy & Gail Chapman.

Our grandchildren - Lesley & Maggie; Brian, Julie, & Tyler; Michele & Mallory.

And our great-grandchildren - MaCayla, Carter, Hudson, Annistyn and a new one, Adaline, just recently born on Christmas Eve, 2017.

Special thanks to **Mike & Cay Adams** for assisting me in preparing *"68 Years Behind The Plow"*. Cay did the typing and Mike inserted the pictures as well as prepared it for publishing. They helped make this a special presentation of my personal memories. I appreciate all of their hard work to help me with this project.

As I list these names I think of Hebrews 11:32 where the writer lists the "Hall of Fame" and says, "What more can I say?" and then thinks of many more! Mine, too, is an endless list but I hope that all of us will be among those in God's Hall of Fame and hear the words –

"Well done thou good and faithful servant!"

Chapter 19
My Last Sermon

Introduction-

1. Preachers often think of what their last sermon might be.
2. Of course, any sermon could be the last. Life is uncertain. My health issues have caused me to give thought to the matter.
3. This lesson has been prepared thinking I might one day be able to present it.

I. Text: Hebrews 4:14 – **Hold Fast**
   A. Always needful and timely – Individuals and congregations
   B. Hebrews was written to Jewish Christians – They were brought up and educated under the law of Moses – were careful to dot "I" and cross "T's" Truly devout – But when Jesus came they began to see the fulfillment of O.T. prophecy in Him. Those who were honest became Christians.
      1. <u>What happened?</u> Persecution (discuss) – Many recanted and returned to the Law of Moses – Others were on the verge.
   C. Book written to: encourage - comfort - strengthen – prevent further apostasy!
   If you have ever been discouraged – stressed – weak – need message of Hebrews – **Hold Fast!!**

II. <u>Nothing New</u>
   A. Jesus – Matthew 24 – Foretelling destruction of Jerusalem – warns them- tells them to watch – be ready – Hold Fast
   B. Paul – I Cor. 15:58 – Therefore
   C. Peter – 2 Peter 1 – Christian virtues
   D. James – Chapter 4 – Resist All with One Accord
   E. Jude – v. 21 – <u>HOLD FAST</u>!! - Personal example of Holding on!
   F. John – Rev 2:10

III. Some who failed –
   1. Judas – Acts 1
   2. Ananias and Sapphira – Acts 5
   3. Demas
   4. Church – Gal 1: 6-8

IV. <u>Marshall Keeble</u> – sermon – Take hold – Hold on – Never let go

V. Warnings –Hebrews 3:12 – I Peter 5:8

VI. What can help us hold fast?
   1. One thing – faithfulness
      a. Worship – prayer – Bible Study – Pure Life – James 1:27

Example – Arland Williams – FL plane crash

Religion that God our father
accepts as pure and faultless
is this:
to look after the orphans and
widows in their distress
and keep oneself from being
polluted by the world.

James 1:27 (NIV)

Forrest T. Chapman

Chapman Family Preachers
Listing in the *Preachers of Today* (1952)

FATHER

Chapman, Adair Pinckney, Sr., Route 5, Moultrie, Ga.; HOME CONGREGATION: Lakeview Chapel; BIRTH: Bartow County, Ga., June 20, 1889; BAPTIZED BY: Brother Langford, Aug., 1910; WIFE: Elizabeth Butler, Married: Aug. 16, 1919; CHILDREN: Adair, Jr., 38, Mildred, 34, Forrest, 29, Arlin, 24; BEGAN PREACHING: Colquitt County, Ga., 1918, regular work in 1924; COLLEGES: Second District Agricultural College, David Lipscomb College, Mercer University; CHURCHES SERVED: Moultrie, 1924-28, 1933-35, 1941-49, Albany, 1924-28, Morven, 1924-28, Cordele, 1950-51, Lakeview Chapel, 1958-59, Various other mission points in Georgia; MEETINGS: Dawson, Ga., Blue Ridge, Ga., Lakeview Chapel near Moultrie, Ga.; PERMANENT CONTACT: Mrs. A. P. Chapman, Route 5, Moultrie, Ga.; OTHER FACTS: Religious Debates, Chapman-Johnson, "Apostasy", Radio, Moultrie, Ga., and Cordele, Ga. Have also engaged in farming and cattle raising. Have done extensive mission work in South Georgia since 1918. Three sons are preachers, Adair, Jr., Forrest and Arlin.

OLDEST SON

Chapman, Adair Pinckney, Jr.

5501 Richmond Ave., Dallas, Tex.; BIRTH: Berlin, Ga., Mar. 7, 1921; WIFE: Nancy Mullaney; CHILDREN: Two; BAPTIZED BY: Houstin Itin, Dec., 1939; BEGAN PREACHING: Searcy, Ark., 1940; TRAINING: Harding College, University of Georgia Law School, Arkansas State Teacher's College; CHURCHES SERVED: Waverly Avenue, Kansas City, Kan., 1943-45, Clements Street, Paducah, Ky., 1949-50, Highland Park, Dallas, Tex., 1951-; RADIO: Paducah, Ky.; MEETINGS PER YEAR: Three; PERMANENT CONTACT: A. P. Chapman, Sr., Rt. 5, Moultrie, Ga.; OTHER FACTS OF INTEREST: From 1945 to 1949 worked under the West End congregation in Atlanta in establishing the church in Athens, Ga.

MIDDLE SON

Chapman, Forrest Tyndall, 479 King Arnold St., Hapeville, Ga.; HOME CONGREGATION: North Avenue; BIRTH: Moultrie, Ga., Sept. 12, 1929; BAPTIZED BY: Adair P. Chapman, Aug., 1941; WIFE: Burma Yelverton, Married: Mar. 17, 1952; CHILDREN: Forrest Tyndall, Jr., 6, Katrina Cay, 3; BEGAN PREACHING: Vicinity of Harding College, 1948; COLLEGES: Harding College, David Lipscomb College, 1949-50, B.A.; CHURCHES SERVED: Highland Avenue, Albany, Ga., 1950-53, River Street, Valdosta, Ga., 1954-56, North Avenue, Hapeville, Ga., 1957—; MEETINGS: Braddock Road, Alexandria, Va., Park Boulevard, Louisville, Ky., Broad Street, Albertville, Ala., MacDill Avenue,

YOUNGEST SON

Chapman, Charles Arlin, 100 Wingfield, Rome, Ga.; HOME CONGREGATION: Rome; BIRTH: Moultrie, Ga., 1935; BAPTIZED BY: J. P. Prevatt, June, 1950; WIFE: Doris Romelta Walker. Married: Dec. 20, 1956; BEGAN PREACHING: Searcy, Ark., 1953; COLLEGES: Harding College, Florida Christian College; CHURCHES SERVED: Highland Park, Dallas, Tex., summers of 1955-56, Lake Dallas, Tex., 1956-57, Wood Street, Denton, Tex., 1957-59, Rome, Ga., 1959—; MEETINGS: Southwest City, Mo., Reedyville, Ky., Lake Dallas, Tex., Olla, La., Wood Street, Denton, Tex.; PERMANENT CONTACT: Mr. and Mrs. Adair P. Chapman, Route 5, Moultrie, Ga.; OTHER FACTS: Father and two brothers are also preachers. Father has been preaching for about 37 years and has worked in several mission points on South Georgia, and also with more established congregations in the same state.

FAREWELL:

"And now, brethren, I commend you to God, and to the word of his grace, which is able to build you up, and to give you an inheritance among all them which are sanctified."

Paul, the apostle
Acts 20:32

Made in the USA
Las Vegas, NV
26 April 2021